D1255032

Recipe FOR A Book Club

A Monthly Guide *for* Hosting Your Own Reading Group

Menus & Recipes, Featured Authors,
Suggested Readings, and Topical Questions

by Mary O'Hare *and* Rose Storey

CAPITAL
BOOKS, INC.
Sterling, Virginia

Capital Books, Inc.
P.O. Box 605
Herndon, Virginia 20172-0605

ISBN 1-931868-83-2 (alk.paper)

Library of Congress Cataloging-in-Publication Data

O'Hare, Mary.
    Recipe for a book club : a monthly guide for hosting your own reading group menus & recipes, featured authors,
        suggested readings and topical questions / by Mary O'Hare and Rose Storey.
        p. cm.
    Includes index.
    ISBN 1-931868-83-2
        1. Cookery. 2. Menus. 3. Book clubs (Discussion groups) I. Storey, Rose. II. Title.

TX714.O345 2004
642'.4--dc22

                                                                                            2004007582

Designed by Rose Storey

Printed in Canada on acid-free paper that meets the American National Standards Institute Z39-48 Standard.

First Edition

10 9 8 7 6 5 4 3 2 1

This book is dedicated with appreciation to our husbands,

Ken Storey and Tom O'Hare.

And to our parents, Gene and Betty Skazinski, whose love of

books and gracious hospitality inspired us.

Contents

Introduction

Reading a good book provides as much mental nourishment as eating a good meal. Sharing a book and a meal with family and friends is a rewarding way to nourish the body and soul. A book club provides variety in reading selections and an opportunity for lively discussion. In addition to broadening your literary knowledge, it can serve to expand your culinary perspective. **RECIPE FOR A BOOK CLUB** suggests menus and themes for hosting your book club meetings. Our intent is to help you create a relaxed atmosphere and minimize the stress that individuals often feel when they host a gathering. The menus included can also be used for any social occasion. Perhaps you already belong to a book club but, if not, here are some suggestions and guidelines that will help you to form your own.

What we have found is that you need at least four people for a book club to function successfully. With four members you can host the meetings two or three times a year and not feel burdened by the task. Finding others interested in a book club doesn't have to be difficult. You can promote membership in community or association newsletters, church and school publications, and home or office communications. What you'll most likely discover is that many people are looking for a book club to join, and it is doubtful that you will have only four members for very long. The ideal number for a book club is six to ten members. That way if someone is absent, you will still have enough attendees for lively discussions and interesting meetings, yet remain a small enough group for all to participate.

RECIPE FOR A BOOK CLUB features a recommended book a month, along with a brief synopsis, book review, author biography, additional book titles, and discussion questions at the end of each chapter. Each month has a different theme, the idea being to encourage a variety of genres to explore as a group.

It is best to hold meetings once a month with members rotating the hosting duties. They can be held any time of day, depending on what works best for the members as a group. You can begin your meetings at any time of year. We used January as our starting date for practical reasons.

The person hosting the meeting is responsible for providing the meal or snacks depending on the time of day your meeting is held. **RECIPE FOR A BOOK CLUB** has a variety of menus that can be modified with additions or deletions depending on when you host the meeting.

As everyone arrives, have a beverage to serve and one or two munchies out. Discussion of the book should begin once the majority of members are present. Usually forty-five minutes to an hour is sufficient time to discuss the book. Remember you are not writing a review for the *New York Times*! You are here to enjoy yourself and the company of others, and discuss a book you have all read.

Now, let the reading and eating begin!

January

DEBUT BOOKS

> "In the meantime, I bought us lunch at McDonald's, and from the way Violet ate, I could tell it was her first hot meal in a while."
>
> **ANGEL STRINGS** by GARY EBERLE

This fast-paced book is about a man's personal revelations through the experiences he has with people he encounters during a cross-country trip. Joe Findaly, who narrates the story, is the hero in search of something more fulfilling in his life than just performing as a backup guitarist in Las Vegas. His whole life changes when he agrees to drive Violet, a hitchhiker, and her baby to San Diego. The only problem is he's on his way to New York City to audition as a guitarist with a rock band. Despite that fact he now finds himself headed west!

Suggestion

We think this is the perfect time to ring in the new year focusing on an author's first book. Your local library is an excellent source when searching for new book titles and suggestions. Another great way to learn about new books is to invite a local bookstore owner to your meeting. Many owners welcome the opportunity to share their newfound authors, plus, this provides them with an opportunity to generate more business. You may even want to inquire about group discounts for your club—it's a great way to support your local bookstore.

Menu

SERVES FOUR TO SIX

Red Wine

Mushroom Bruschetta

Tomato and Fresh Mozzarella Salad

Snow Pasta

Pistachio Cake

Our Review

ANGEL STRINGS by GARY EBERLE

This book is a fun read because it is filled with zany, hilarious, and colorful characters. The author uses a

road trip in a van as a means to transport his characters from one adventure to another. Joe, the driver of the

van, is a congenial person searching for some meaning in his life. He narrates his encounters and experiences

with wry and touching observations. At times his experiences are mind-boggling. Once Joe starts the van,

you won't want to get out. ANGEL STRINGS is a fun read.

About the Author

Gary Eberle is chairman of the English department at Aquinas College in Grand Rapids, Michigan, where he

has been honored by both the Student Senate and faculty. ANGEL STRINGS is his first novel. He has also

written a nonfiction book and a collection of short stories.

Suggested Readings

THE FOURTH ANGEL by SUZANNE CHAZIN

"The food came and Marenko made a brave stab at using the chopsticks..."

IN THE COMPANY OF ANGELS by N. M. KELBY

"...I heard the butcher found a small cross within the belly of a lamb."

THE GOOD PEOPLE OF NEW YORK by THISBE NISSEN

"...she'd retreated for a few moments of reprieve under the pretense of replenishing the bean dip."

AUTUMN CLOUD by JACKIE BONG WRIGHT

"She hired laborers to plant soya, corn, beans, peas, sugar cane, and fruit trees."

THE MIRACLE LIFE OF EDGAR MINT by BRADY UDALL

"...the dinner rolls shrank, milk was withheld, dessert went missing, all of which put the food I regularly stole from the storage rooms in higher demand."

BOY STILL MISSING by JOHN SEARLES

"...I'd shove my sweatshirt pockets full of maraschino cherries and a couple of green olives..."

Mushroom Bruschetta

2 Tbs	Olive oil
2 tsp	Butter
3/4 lb	Mushrooms, finely chopped
3 cloves	Garlic, minced
1/4 tsp	Salt
1/8 tsp	Pepper
1/4 tsp	Dried sage
1 Tbs	Fresh parsley, chopped
1	Tomato, seeded and finely chopped
1 loaf	Baguette, sliced
1 cup	Finely shredded mozzarella

In a large frying pan, heat the olive oil and butter over moderately high heat. Add the mushrooms, garlic, salt, pepper, and sage. Cook, stirring occasionally, until the mushrooms are golden, 5 to 10 minutes. Stir in the parsley and tomato. Remove from the heat.

Spread the mixture onto the baguette slices. Sprinkle a small amount of mozzarella on each piece. Place in 375-degree oven for 5 to 7 minutes, or just until warm.

Can also be served at room temperature.

"I took some woodbine that was growing there and ate some of it so it'd get in my milk for the baby."

ANGEL STRINGS by GARY EBERLE

our notes:

When cleaning mushrooms, brush off the top layer— never rinse in water.

The topping may be prepared a day in advance, then reheated in the microwave before placing on a baguette slice.

your notes:

Tomato & Fresh Mozzarella salad

6 Tbs	Olive oil
2 Tbs	Italian dressing
1 tsp	Dried basil
1 tsp	Oregano
1 pound	Fresh mozzarella, sliced
2 Tbs	White wine vinegar
2	Tomatoes, sliced
	Fresh basil leaves

Create a marinade with the olive oil, dressing, basil, and oregano. Marinate the mozzarella overnight.

An hour or 2 before the gathering, alternate the mozzarella and tomato slices on a circular platter. Use the basil leaves as decoration in the middle and place some across the top of the mozzarella and tomato slices.

"I rolled my eyes and pushed the carrot mush away."

"When Violet came out I made her eat some ham and eggs."

ANGEL STRINGS by GARY EBERLE

our notes:

Plum tomatoes are a nice size for slicing and display.

Fresh mozzarella can usually be found in round form in the deli section of a grocery store.

your notes:

Snow Pasta

1/2 lb	Penne pasta
2 Tbs	Olive oil
2 Tbs	Lemon juice
2 cloves	Garlic, crushed
6 oz	Firm tofu, finely chopped
1/4 cup	Finely chopped onion
1 tsp	Basil
1/2 tsp	Salt
1/2 tsp	Pepper
1 can (7 oz)	Mushrooms
1 can (15 oz)	Sliced black olives
2 tubs (8 oz ea)	Pesto sauce
1/4 cup	Parmesan cheese

Cook and drain pasta.

Heat olive oil, lemon juice, and garlic. Add tofu, onion, basil, salt, pepper, mushrooms, and black olives. Sauté on low heat for about 15 to 20 minutes. Turn off fire and add pesto sauce and noodles, mixing gently. Place in dish and sprinkle with Parmesan cheese.

"...Violet piled four cream-filled donuts, a big glass of orange juice, and a sprite on her tray."

ANGEL STRINGS by GARY EBERLE

our notes:

The tofu is an unusual and healthy surprise.

This can be made before your guests arrive, then kept covered with foil in a warm oven.

your notes:

Pistachio Cake

2 pkgs	Pistachio pudding mix, divided
1 pkg	White cake mix
3/4 cup	Sliced almonds, divided
3	Eggs
1 cup	Ginger ale
3/4 cup	Vegetable oil
1 1/2 tsp	Almond extract
1 container (12 oz)	Cool Whip
1/4 cup	Milk

Cake:

Using an electric mixer, combine 1 package pistachio pudding mix, white cake mix, 1/2 cup almonds, eggs, ginger ale, vegetable oil, and almond extract. Pour into two lightly greased 8-inch cake pans. Bake at 325 degrees for 30 minutes or until toothpick inserted in center comes out clean. Cool.

Frosting:

Mix together 1 package pistachio pudding mix, Cool Whip, and milk. After frosting, decorate with remaining 1/4 cup almonds.

Refrigerate until ready to serve.

"...and we had some baloney sandwiches for lunch..."

ANGEL STRINGS by GARY EBERLE

our notes:

This cake is so moist and delicious—you can't go wrong!

When frosting, you may also want to sprinkle a few almonds in between the two layers.

your notes:

Questions

ONE

Discuss what kind of childhoods you think Joe and Violet had.

TWO

If you could describe Joe's personality in one or two words, what would they be?

THREE

What was the most preposterous event in the book?

FOUR

Who, in your opinion, was the least believable character?

FIVE

Do you think that Joe and Violet lived "happily ever after"?

February

CLASSICS AND ROMANCE

"We have dined nine times at Rosing's..."

PRIDE AND PREJUDICE by JANE AUSTEN

This is a story about Elizabeth Bennet, her four sisters, and their numerous suitors. Set in eighteenth-century England, the novel introduces the manners and customs of genteel society of the day. It is at a ball that Elizabeth first encounters the proud Mr. Darcy, who neglects to ask her to dance. Her pride, offended at this rejection, causes her to initially judge him harshly and unfavorably. The story follows Mr. Darcy's courtship of Elizabeth, but along the way we meet a rogue, a lovesick sister, society snobs, and numerous other memorable characters who combine to make this a story you won't soon forget.

Suggestion

Since you will be serving a variety of finger sandwiches, we suggest you make three to four of each type for your guests and yourself. To serve the tea sandwiches, place one of each type on individual plates for each guest and the extras on a large platter to pass around.

A nice touch is to fill candy dishes with tiny heart-shape candies and splurge on some flowers.

Menu

SERVES FOUR TO SIX

Champagne

A Variety of Finger Sandwiches: Olive Nut,

Cucumber, Crab, and Chicken

Lemon Cake with Darjeeling Tea

Our Review

PRIDE AND PREJUDICE by JANE AUSTEN

PRIDE AND PREJUDICE is a charming portrait of life in late eighteenth-century England. Despite the passage of more than two centuries since the book's publication, one is still able to identify with many of the characters. Jane Austen's precise verbal portraits allow us a glimpse into the life and times of the society of that age. Once you get "into it," you'll be hooked!

About the Author

Jane Austen was born in Southern England on December 16, 1775. Of the eight children, Jane was the second daughter and seventh eldest. Her father was a rector with a modest income, which he supplemented by tutoring. As a child, Jane briefly attended a boarding school with her sister, Cassandra, but for the most part her education at home comprised the genteel arts of music, language study, and drawing. She enjoyed reading serious literature as well as popular novels.

Jane originally wrote to entertain her family. The first novel she sold to a publisher, **NORTHANGER ABBEY,** was not published for several years but she continued to write.

Upon her father's retirement, the family moved to Bath, where they remained until his death in 1805. Neither she nor her sister ever married, and with the death of their father, their income was reduced. Jane, her sister Cassandra, and their mother were dependent on her brothers for support. She continued to write, and it was during this time that several of her novels were published, and her writings gained popularity. **PRIDE AND PREJUDICE** was sold to a publisher in 1812.

Jane was unwell the last few years of her life, and it is suspected that she suffered from Addison's disease. She died on July 18, 1817, at the age of forty-one.

Suggested Readings

IVANHOE by SIR WALTER SCOTT

"...took from the larger board a mess of pottage and seethed kid..."

VANITY FAIR by WILLIAM MAKEPEACE THACKERAY

"At the rectory...the young ladies had each a glass from a bottle of currant wine."

DAVID COPPERFIELD by CHARLES DICKENS

"...we had sandwiches and wine and water."

TESS OF THE D'URBERVILLES by THOMAS HARDY

"His mother made him sandwiches..."

BARCHESTER TOWERS by ANTHONY TROLLOPE

"The Bishop of Barchester said grace over the well-spread board in the Ullathorne dining-room;"

PERE GORIOT by HONORÉ DE BALZAC

"...and it would be much better for you to give us some of your Bordeaux,..."

Olive Nut Filling

Combine:

6 oz	Cream cheese, softened (brick style)
1/2 cup	Mayonnaise

Add to that:

1/2 cup	Chopped pecans
1 cup	Chopped pimento-stuffed green olives
	Dash of pepper

Thinly sliced white bread

Garnish: Watercress and cherry tomato

On the day of the meeting:
Cut rectangular-shape pieces from slices of white bread, two pieces per slice of bread. Spread with filling and garnish with small piece of watercress and cherry tomato half.

"Who could have imagined that we should receive an invitation to dine there..."

"...both Kitty and Lydia looking out of a dining-room up stairs."

PRIDE AND PREJUDICE by JANE AUSTEN

our notes:

The filling needs to be refrigerated for several hours or overnight.

We suggest Pepperidge Farm white bread, with the crusts trimmed off.

your notes:

Cucumber Sandwiches

1	Seedless cucumber, thinly sliced
2 Tbs	White wine vinegar
1 bunch	Radishes, thinly sliced
	Whipped butter
	Salt and white pepper, to taste

Thinly sliced white bread.

Garnish: Parsley

Slice cucumber very thin using a vegetable peeler. Place in a shallow dish, sprinkle with vinegar, salt, and pepper. Let stand a few hours or overnight.

On the day of the meeting:
Using cookie cutter, if desired, cut out heart shapes from the bread. Butter the bread. Drain cucumber slices and place on paper towel. Place a cucumber on the bread first, then a radish, and garnish with parsley.

"...they triumphantly displayed a table set out with such cold meat as an inn larder usually affords..."

PRIDE AND PREJUDICE by JANE AUSTEN

our notes:

Rinse and dry the cucumber before slicing, since you won't be removing the green peel.

Again, we would suggest Pepperidge Farm white bread with the crusts removed.

your notes:

Crab Rounds

1 can (6 oz)	Crabmeat
1/2 cup	Mayonnaise
2 Tbs	Cream cheese (brick)
1/2 tsp	Dried onion
1 tsp	Lemon juice
1/2 tsp	Season-All®

Combine all ingredients and refrigerate overnight.

Thinly sliced white bread, crusts trimmed off

Garnish: Black olives, sliced

On the day of the meeting:
Using a round cookie cutter, cut bread into circles or "rounds."
Place crab filling on bread and garnish with slices of black olives.

Chicken Sandwiches

2 cups	Cooked and diced chicken
1/2 cup	Mayonnaise
1 stalk	Celery, finely chopped
1/2 tsp	Dried onions
1/2 tsp	Season-All®

Combine. This may be prepared ahead and refrigerated overnight.

Thinly sliced white bread, crusts trimmed off

Garnish: Sweet mini gherkins, thinly sliced

On the day of the meeting:
Cut bread in desired shape, spread with filling, and garnish with
thinly sliced gherkins.

our notes:

Rinse the crabmeat in a colander with cold water and press out excess water with a fork. Use a firm white or wheat bread for the crab.

Try a heartier bread for the chicken—pumpernickel, whole wheat, or seven-grain is delicious.

your notes:

Lemon Cake

1 cup	Sweet Butter, softened
2 cups	Sugar
3	Eggs

Cream together butter and sugar and beat in eggs, one at a time.

Combine:

3 cups	Flour
1 tsp	Baking powder
1/4 tsp	Salt

Gradually add flour mixture to the butter, sugar, and egg mixture alternating with **1 cup heavy whipping cream**. Begin and end with the flour combination.

Add **3 Tbs of lemon juice** and **1 Tbs grated lemon zest**.
Bake at 300 degrees in a greased and floured tube pan. Bake for 1 hour or until done; test with toothpick to see if it comes out clean. Cool for about 20 to 30 minutes in the pan, then remove to serving plate to finish cooling.

Glaze:

1/4 cup soft butter blended with 1 1/2 cups of powdered sugar and 3 tbs of lemon juice. Drizzle over the cooled cake.

"...where Miss Bennet was making tea and Elizabeth pouring out the coffee..."

PRIDE AND PREJUDICE by JANE AUSTEN

our notes:

You may substitute buttermilk for the heavy whipping cream.

For lemon zest:
Wash and dry a lemon and use a fine shredder to grate the skin.

your notes:

Questions

PRIDE AND PREJUDICE by JANE AUSTEN

ONE

Considering your first impression of Mr. Darcy, was Elizabeth justified in her opinion of him?

TWO

Given the different personalities of Mr. and Mrs. Bennet, did their respective interests

influence the behaviors of their daughters?

THREE

Just for fun….what kind of careers would each of the Bennet girls have if they lived today?

FOUR

What were some of the reservations about Elizabeth and her family that Mr. Darcy

had to overcome to finally propose marriage to her?

FIVE

PRIDE AND PREJUDICE introduces the reader to persons that represent various social classes.

If you were a character in this book, which class would you most likely be identified with, and

how comfortable would you be living in that type of environment?

March

HERITAGE

"...the Russians gave her fresh loaves of bread from their army bakery, because we could eat the bread right away without additional processing or trading."

GERMAN BOY by WOLFGANG W. E. SAMUEL

This is a true story about a German family at the end of World War II. The narrator, ten-year-old Wolfgang Samuel, tells of his mother's resourcefulness and the sacrifices she made to ensure her family's survival at the close of the war.

suggestion

For those of you who wish to acknowledge St. Patrick's Day, we've included a recipe for Irish Sweet Bread for you to prepare for each of your guests to take home.

Menu

SERVES FOUR TO SIX

Irish Sweet Bread

Snakebites

Spinach and Artichoke Appetizer

Asparagus Salad with Chilled Salmon

Crusty French Bread

Sour Cream Apple Squares

Our Review

GERMAN BOY by WOLFGANG W. E. SAMUEL

The finely detailed portraits of people Wolfgang encountered and historical events he experienced puts you right into the heart of the conflict. His descriptions are simple and clear, and this youngster's poignant voice during war will keep you transfixed throughout.

Wolfgang Samuel's vivid and moving descriptions of life as a German refugee will immerse you in the horrors of war and its aftermath. Despite all of its sadness, the story is one of joy, hope, dedication, and personal triumph.

About the Author

Wolfgang Samuel was born in Germany in 1935. He moved to Colorado in 1951 with his mother and her second husband, Leo Ferguson. Wolfgang served in the United States Air Force for thirty years, retiring in 1985 with the rank of Colonel. He is also the author of **I ALWAYS WANTED TO FLY**.

Suggested Readings

HUNGRY FOR HOME by COLE MORTON

"she had made me a sandwich with thick ham from a waxed-paper packet..."

THE TORTILLA CURTAIN by T. CORAGHESSAN BOYLE

"...six slices of toast in the shining silver toaster,
eggs and a slab of ham..."

IN CUBA I WAS A GERMAN SHEPHERD by ANA MENENDEZ

"...a generation of former professors served black beans and rice to the nostalgic."

MEMOIRS OF A GEISHA by ARTHUR S. GOLDEN

"...I find tea ceremony as enjoyable as a good night's sleep."

ANGELA'S ASHES by FRANK McCOURT

"I wish I had something to eat..."

THE RED TENT by ANITA DIAMANT

"she tried to tempt her with her favorite sweets but Rachel spat at the food, and
at Leah, who seemed to grow bigger and rounder every day..."

Irish Sweet Bread

2 1/4 cups	Flour
1/2 cup	Raisins
2 1/4 tsp	Baking powder
1/4 tsp	Baking soda
3/4 tsp	Salt
3/4–1 cup	Sugar
1	Egg
2 Tbs	Oil
3/4 cup	Milk
1 Tbs	Caraway seeds (optional)

Garnish: Sugar

Preheat oven to 350 degrees. Place flour in bowl, then toss the raisins until they are covered with flour. Add the rest of the dry ingredients and mix well. With a wire whisk mix egg, oil, and milk in a separate bowl. Add to flour mixture and stir just until blended. Fold in caraway seeds. Pour into a greased and floured 9 x 5-inch loaf pan. Sprinkle some sugar on top. Bake 55 to 60 minutes till done.

"It would be our major food source for the winter..."

GERMAN BOY by WOLFGANG W. E. SAMUEL

our notes:

Use small disposable loaf pans available at the grocery store (makes two loaves per recipe).

your notes:

snakebites

Mix equal parts of Harp Lager (beer) and hard apple cider in a pint glass or other type of fancy beer glass.

spinach & Artichoke Appetizer

1 pkg (10 oz)	Frozen chopped spinach, thawed
1 can (14 oz)	Artichoke hearts, drained and chopped
1/2 cup	Mayonnaise
1/2 cup	Parmesan cheese
1 tsp	Onion powder
1 tsp	Garlic powder
1/2 tsp	Pepper
1 pkg (17.3 oz)	Frozen puff pastry

Drain spinach well, pressing between layers of paper towels. Stir together spinach, artichoke, and next five ingredients.

Thaw puff pastry at room temperature 30 minutes. Unfold and place on floured surface. Spread spinach mixture on pastry, leaving 1/2-inch border. Roll up "jelly roll" fashion. Seal seam by pinching lightly. Wrap in plastic and freeze 30 minutes. Cut into 1/2-inch slices. When ready to use, place desired number of appetizers on lightly greased cookie sheet.

Bake at 400 degrees for 10 minutes on each side. Remove when golden brown.

our notes:

If your guests prefer not to try the lager, cider is delicious alone.

The spinach and artichoke rolls can be frozen for up to three months.

your notes:

Chilled Salmon

2 lbs   Fresh salmon

Spray a 9 x 13-inch pan with Pam, then place salmon (skin side down) in pan.

Combine and sprinkle the following on the salmon:

     Juice of 1 lemon

3 Tbs   White wine

1/2 tsp   Seasoned salt

1/2 tsp   Garlic

2 Tbs   Melted butter

Bake at 350 degrees for approximately 25 minutes until done (salmon should flake when tested with a fork). Remove from pan and refrigerate. When chilled, remove the skin and return to the refrigerator. Serve with Asparagus Salad on next page.

"Usually Ingrid got to eat the rice, because Oma claimed that she didn't like rice, and instead preferred eating potatoes dipped in salt..."

GERMAN BOY by WOLFGANG W. E. SAMUEL

our notes:

The salmon may be prepared a day in advance.

your notes:

Asparagus salad

1 lb   Fresh asparagus, cut into 2-inch lengths.
Steam for about 8 minutes till tender but firm. Cool completely.

1   Hard-boiled egg, chopped
1   Tomato, sliced

Salad "fixins":
8 cups   Torn lettuce
1 cup   Chopped celery
1/4 cup   Sliced green onions

Dressing:
Combine the following:
1/2 cup   Salad oil
1/4 cup   Finely chopped canned pickled beets
2 Tbs   White wine vinegar
2 Tbs   Lemon juice
1 tsp   Sugar
1 tsp   Salt
1 tsp   Paprika
1/2 tsp   Dry mustard
4 drops   Tabasco sauce

Toss salad "fixins" and asparagus gently and place on individual plates. Sprinkle about 1 tsp of chopped egg on each salad. Place a slice of salmon on top of the salad and garnish with slice of ripe tomato.

Serve with crusty french bread.

our notes:

Be sure not to overcook the asparagus.

Any lettuce will do, but we prefer a combination such as leafy green and Boston.

Dressing can be prepared a day or two in advance.

your notes:

Sour Cream Apple Squares

2 cups	Brown sugar
2 cups	Flour
1/2 cup	Butter, softened
1 cup	Chopped nuts

Combine first 3 ingredients in a large bowl until fine crumbs form; stir in nuts. Press 2 3/4 cups of mixture into ungreased 13 x 9-inch pan, pressing the mixture in firmly.

To remaining crumb mixture add:

1 to 2 tsp	Cinnamon
1 tsp	Baking soda
1/2 tsp	Salt
1	Egg
1 cup	Sour cream
1 tsp	Vanilla

Combine all ingredients together in a large bowl and blend well. Add to that **2 cups finely chopped apples** (Granny Smith or other baking apple) and stir into batter.

Bake at 350 degrees for 30 to 40 minutes.

Serve with whipped cream or vanilla ice cream.

"...a thick noodle soup with pieces of chicken floating in it."

GERMAN BOY by WOLFGANG W. E. SAMUEL

our notes:

For St. Patrick's Day, sprinkle a tiny amount of green sugar crystals on topping just before serving.

your notes:

Questions

GERMAN BOY by WOLFGANG W. E. SAMUEL

ONE

As the story unfolds, one gets the impression that Hedy was in denial about the progress of the war.

What do you think?

TWO

Ingrid, Wolfgang's sister, when mentioned throughout the book, appears quiet and withdrawn.

What do you think her thoughts and fears were, and how was she coping with them?

THREE

How would you describe Hedy's personality?

Do you think these trials brought out the best in her?

FOUR

What are some of your memories as a ten-year-old?

FIVE

Why do you think the Russians were so undisciplined and cruel

compared to most of the other allies?

April

AMERICAN LIVES

"At Christmas, we'd serve coffee, fruit, and waffles with whipped cream all day long, until no one could eat anymore."

HAVING OUR SAY by SARAH L. DELANY AND A. ELIZABETH DELANY
WITH AMY HILL HEARTH

This is an oral history recounted by two women who lived from the horse-and-buggy age to the jet age. Bessie and Sadie Delany had professional occupations at a time when most women, especially young black women, had very little education. We hear in their own words the history of their family and the experiences of their youth, which included attending school at St. Augustine's in Raleigh, North Carolina, working in Harlem, and having experiences which led to long-term success despite all odds.

Suggestion

Ask your guests to bring a picture of a relative who was born at or near the turn of the century.
Does your guest have any interesting stories about this person?

Menu

SERVES FOUR TO SIX

Iced Tea with Fresh Fruit

Vegetable Squares

Corn Pudding

Orange and Almond Chicken Salad

Peaches and Cream

Our Review

HAVING OUR SAY by SARAH L. DELANY AND A. ELIZABETH DELANY
WITH AMY HILL HEARTH

The Delany sisters recount the story of their life in witty, candid observations that reveal the lives of two

remarkable women. Their parents, one of whom was a slave, were born before emancipation in 1863,

but they were both educated and eventually became respected teachers and administrators of

St. Augustine's College in Raleigh, North Carolina. Because of their parents' guidance and advice,

Sadie and Bessie, as well as their eight siblings, became respected and influential members of their

communities. You will learn much about American history from the perspective of the Delany sisters.

About the Author

Amy Hill Hearth is a former journalist who has written frequently for the *New York Times*. During the several

months she spent working closely with Sadie and Bessie Delany, she became close friends with both sisters

and collaborated on several more projects related to **HAVING OUR SAY**. Ms. Hearth lives in New Jersey.

Suggested Readings

JOHN ADAMS by DAVID McCULLOUGH

*"Sunday dinners, served at one o'clock, he remembered
as sufficiently plentiful but modest..."*

PLAINSONG by KENT HARUF

*"...when they entered the kitchen he was standing at the gas stove
stirring eggs in a black cast-iron skillet."*

THE THINGS THEY CARRIED by TIM O'BRIEN

*"...picking up little phrases of Vietnamese, learning how to cook rice over a can of
sterno, how to eat with her hands."*

AUTOBIOGRAPHY OF BEN FRANKLIN by BENJAMIN FRANKLIN

"I had made many a meal on bread..."

LINCOLN: A NOVEL by GORE VIDAL

"The family was seated at the breakfast table..."

EMPIRE FALLS by RICHARD RUSSO

*"He set up Horace's platter with tomato, lettuce, a slice of Bermuda onion
and a pickle, plus the open-faced bun..."*

Iced Tea with Fresh Fruit

2 quarts	Boiling water
4	Tea bags
1 cup	Sugar

Place tea in pot, pour boiling water over it, and let steep for
5 to 10 minutes. Remove tea bags and add sugar, stirring until it
dissolves completely. Once the tea has cooled, transfer to a pitcher
and refrigerate.

To serve:
Using tall tumblers, place ice in half the glass. Add a few pieces of
fresh fruit, then pour tea over the fruit and serve.

"I could not get enough to eat. Mama was
so worried that she fixed a small basket
of food each morning for me to carry with
me all day..."

HAVING OUR SAY
by SARAH L. DELANY AND A. ELIZABETH DELANY
WITH AMY HILL HEARTH

our notes:

Earl Grey tea is always
a favorite.

We suggest using
raspberries or peaches for
an exceptional flavor.

your notes:

Vegetable Squares

2 cans (8 oz each) Crescent dinner rolls

Place crescent rolls flat on a jelly roll-size cookie sheet and bake at
375 degrees until lightly browned, about 10 minutes. Cool.

1 pkg (8 oz)	Cream cheese, softened
1/2 cup	Sour cream
1 tsp	Dill weed
1/8 tsp	Garlic powder
	Vegetables, chopped or grated

Mix ingredients together and spread on cooled crescent rolls.
Place chopped or grated vegetables on top of mixture. Choose the
vegetables for texture and color, for example, broccoli, cauliflower,
carrots, cucumber, tomatoes, or radishes. Cut into bite-size squares.

"In the morning, he would go out and shoot
a squirrel for his breakfast."

"...so she would take us on the trolley car to
Johnson's drugstore for a limeade, or bring
back some candy..."

HAVING OUR SAY
by SARAH L. DELANY AND A. ELIZABETH DELANY
WITH AMY HILL HEARTH

our notes:

The rolls and vegetables can
be prepared in the morning
but should not be assembled
until shortly before serving.

your notes:

Corn Pudding

1 1/2 cups	Niblets corn, fresh, frozen, or canned
	(drain canned corn)
1 can (15 oz)	Creamed corn
1 cup	Sour cream
1 stick	Butter, melted
2	Eggs, beaten
1/4 cup	Sugar

Mix together.

In a separate bowl combine the following to create the cornmeal mixture:

1 cup	Stone-ground cornmeal
1 cup	Flour
3 Tbs	Baking powder
1 tsp	Salt

Add cornmeal mixture to corn mixture. Place in a greased
9 x 13-inch pan and bake at 350 degrees for about 40 minutes
until golden brown.

*"I would make money on the side by baking
cakes and selling them for a nickel a slice
to the teachers at school."*

HAVING OUR SAY
by SARAH L. DELANY AND A. ELIZABETH DELANY
WITH AMY HILL HEARTH

our notes:

To save time, you can use
Jiffy Corn Muffin Mix in place
of the cornmeal mixture.

Butter or honey is a nice
accompaniment to the
corn pudding.

your notes:

Orange & Almond Chicken Salad

Chicken:

4	Boneless, skinless chicken breasts
1 cup	Italian dressing

Place chicken in a shallow pan. Pour 1 cup of Italian dressing over the chicken and marinate several hours. Transfer to baking dish that has been brushed with olive oil. Bake in preheated oven set at 350 degrees. Cook 20 to 30 minutes, turning once, till done. Remove from oven and refrigerate. Once the chicken is cool, cut it julienne style.

Almonds:

1 cup	Sliced almonds
6 tsp	Sugar

In a small pan cook the almonds and sugar over medium heat, stirring constantly. Once the sugar has melted, remove from heat. Transfer almonds to a plate to cool. When cool, break apart to serve.

Salad:

1/2 head	Iceberg lettuce, torn into bite-size pieces
1/2 head	Romaine lettuce, torn into bite-size pieces
4	Scallions, thinly sliced
1 cup	Celery, cut into bite-size pieces
1 can (15 oz)	Mandarin oranges, drained

Dressing:

1/2 cup	Salad oil
4 Tbs	Sugar
1/2 cup	Red wine vinegar
1 tsp	Salt
1 Tbs	Pepper
3 Tbs	Snipped parsley

When ready to serve:

Toss the salad with the dressing, then add the almonds. Place salad on serving plates and lay chicken slices on top.

our notes:

The chicken is also delicious grilled.

All of these ingredients can be prepared a day in advance, then assembled right before serving.

your notes:

Peaches & Cream

Preheat oven to 350 degrees.

Mix in a small bowl:

3/4 cup	Flour
1 pkg (3oz)	Vanilla pudding (don't use instant)
1 tsp	Baking powder

Then add:

1	Egg, beaten
1/2 cup	Milk
3 Tbs	Butter, melted

Pour into a greased 8 x 8-inch pan.

1 can (16 oz) Sliced peaches, drained and syrup reserved

Cut peaches into bite-size pieces and place on top of batter.

In a separate bowl mix together:

1/2 cup	Peach juice
1 pkg (8oz)	Cream cheese
1/2 cup	Sugar

Pour over peaches.

Combine:

1 Tbs	Sugar
1/2 tsp	Cinnamon

Sprinkle on top. Bake for 45 minutes. Cool before serving.

Questions

HAVING OUR SAY by SARAH L. DELANY AND A. ELIZABETH DELANY
WITH AMY HILL HEARTH

ONE

What question would you ask Sadie and Bessie if you were interviewing them today?

TWO

Henry and Nanny Delany must have been remarkable parents, given the success of their offspring.

What do you think was their greatest contribution to their children?

THREE

Have you learned anything new about the challenges a black person faced in the past

now that you've read this book?

FOUR

Which sister would you most likely be best friends with, Bessie or Sadie?

FIVE

Two approaches to combating racial injustice were mentioned frequently: militant activism and personal

improvement. Which approach is more beneficial, or are both necessary?

May

MEMOIRS

"...food could be dangerous, especially to those who loved it."

TENDER AT THE BONE: GROWING UP AT THE TABLE by RUTH REICHL

This is an enticing memoir that revolves around cooking, eating, and socializing.
Ruth Reichl reminisces about her youth through early adulthood and how she came
to be a respected and admired food connoisseur.

suggestion

Those of you who are mothers may want to invite your daughters and have them bring a favorite childhood book to the brunch. It might be fun for the daughters to reminisce about their books while the mothers discuss the current book of the month. In addition, you may want to have each mother/daughter bring a dozen cookies, either one of the cookie recipes included or one of their own favorites. We've included our mother's Banana Bread recipe, which is one of our favorites—maybe you'd like to make small loaves and give one to each guest.

Menu

SERVES FOUR TO SIX

Apple Juice, Orange Juice, Mimosas

Hot Cheddar Dip

Fresh Fruit and Dip

Yummy French Toast with Warm Fruit Compote

Filled Sugar Cookies

Meringues

Betty's Banana Bread

Our Review

TENDER AT THE BONE: GROWING UP AT THE TABLE by RUTH REICHL

If you love food, we think you'll thoroughly enjoy Ruth Reichl's creative description of food and everything that can be good and bad about it. This memoir starts by depicting her life growing up in a household with a manic-depressive mother who loved to entertain, but also didn't mind sacrificing the quality of food she served to her guests. In these stories, you experience the pain and agony, and somehow the excitement, of all those involved in planning the parties and those simply attending them.

The memoir continues as Ruth moves through adolescence and into adulthood. She shares with us her countless encounters and education revolving around food, including relationships with her family, friends, and romantic interests. A number of recipes in this book only serious cooks would probably dare attempt, but they look delicious. So if you're feeling adventurous yourself, try some of them.

About the Author

Ruth Reichl was raised in Manhattan and Connecticut. She attended high school in Canada to learn French and then went to the University of Michigan. Reichl is a restaurant critic for the *New York Times* and lives in New York City with her husband and son.

Suggested Readings

LITTLE HOUSE ON THE PRAIRIE by LAURA INGALLS WILDER

"The coffee boiled, the cakes baked, the meat fried, and they all smelled so good..."

LITTLE WOMEN by LOUISA MAY ALCOTT

"In the kitchen reigned confusion and despair..."

TOO CLOSE TO THE FALLS by CATHERINE GILDINER

"For over ten years I never once had a meal at home..."

THE SECRET LIFE OF BEES by SUE MONK KIDD

"...the air grew so quiet I could hear the food being ground up in T. Ray's mouth."

THE JOY LUCK CLUB by AMY TAN

"The hostess had to serve special DYANSYIN Foods to bring good fortune of all kinds..."

A GIRL NAMED ZIPPY by HAVEN KIMMEL

"she carries a bottle with her everywhere she goes..."

Beverages

Serve the juice or mimosas in ice-filled goblets with an orange or apple slice on the rim. Mimosas are made with equal parts orange juice and champagne.

Hot Cheddar Dip

1 cup	Grated sharp cheddar cheese
1 cup	Grated Monterey Jack cheese
1 1/2 cups	Mayonnaise
10 slices	Bacon, cooked crisp and chopped in small pieces
1 tsp	Dry onion
1 tsp	Dry mustard
1 tsp	Accent
2	Egg whites, beaten

Combine all ingredients and pour into a buttered, round soufflé dish. A dish approximately 7 inches across and 3 inches deep is a good size.

Bake at 325 degrees for 30 to 40 minutes. Serve hot with crackers.

Fresh Fruit & Dip

Cream Dip:
One 16-ounce container of sour cream mixed thoroughly with 1/4 cup light brown sugar.

Place bowl of dip on platter and arrange strawberry, pear, apple, etc., slices on platter.

our notes:

Pepperidge Farm Butterfly Crackers are a nice complement to the dip.

The pears or apples used in the fruit dip should be cut and placed on the platter just before serving to prevent them from discoloring.

your notes:

Yummy French Toast with Warm Fruit Compote

12 slices of bakery-style white bread.

Mix together:

4	Eggs
2 cups	Half-and-half
1 tsp	Vanilla
1/2 cup	Sugar

In another bowl mix:

8 oz	Cream cheese
1 tsp	Vanilla
1	Egg
1/4 cup	Sugar

Remove crusts from bread and place 6 slices on a greased 9 x 13-inch pan. Pour half of the egg/half-and-half mixture on the bread slices. Then pour the filling on top the moistened bread. Place the last 6 slices of bread on top and finish with the rest of the egg/half-and-half mixture. Cover with aluminum foil. **Refrigerate overnight.** Keep covered with foil and bake in a preheated 350-degree oven for 30 minutes. Remove cover and bake for 30 minutes more. Let stand 10 minutes.

Fruit Compote:

Use any fruit (fresh or canned), but we suggest peaches for their light flavor. You can also use mixed berries or apples.

4	Fresh peaches, pitted, peeled, and thinly sliced
1/4 cup	Sugar

Place peaches in cooking pan over low heat. Slowly stir in sugar and continue cooking until sugar is dissolved.

Place slice of french toast on individual serving plate and spoon the fruit on the side.

our notes:

The fruit compote can also be prepared the day before and then microwaved to warm it up before serving.

your notes:

Filled Sugar Cookies

1 cup	Softened butter
1 1/2 cups	Confectioners' sugar
1	Egg
1 tsp	Vanilla
1 tsp	Almond extract

Mix thoroughly, then add:

2 1/2 cups	Flour
1 tsp	Baking soda
1 tsp	Cream of tartar

Cover and chill 2 to 3 hours.

1 jar (6–7 oz) Apricot preserves

Heat oven to 375 degrees. Divide dough in half. With a rolling pin, roll each half to 3/16 inch thick on lightly floured cloth. Cut into 3-inch-wide circles. Drop apricot preserves into the center, then fold over so you have a half-moon shape. Pinch lightly to seal. Place on lightly greased baking sheet. Bake about 7 to 8 minutes until lightly browned on edges. Cool on wire rack.

"I turned to the stove and poured the egg and matzo mixture..."

TENDER AT THE BONE by RUTH REICHL

our notes:

If you don't want a fruit filling, you can substitute almond paste (or canned almond filling).

your notes:

Meringues

4	Egg whites
1	Pinch of salt
1 cup	Sugar

Preheat oven to 300 degrees. Beat whites and salt at high speed until soft peaks form. Gradually add sugar, a little at a time, beating until the mixture is stiff and shiny. Drop by teaspoon onto greased cookie sheet. Bake 30 minutes and cool on wire rack.

Makes about 2 dozen cookies.

"...we began cooking Greek food with the olive oil, lamb, and grape leaves we brought home from our expeditions."

"...we were dragging home torn bags of marshmallows, dented cans of soda, and similarly forbidden foods."

TENDER AT THE BONE by RUTH REICHL

our notes:

The meringues are sweet and very delicious with a cup of tea.

your notes:

Betty's Banana Bread

| 1/2 cup | Crisco (or 1 stick [1/2 cup] margarine) |
| 1 1/2 cups | Sugar |

Cream together.

Add:

| 2 | Eggs |
| 3 or 4 | Ripe bananas, mashed |

Alternate, adding to the creamed mixture:

3 cups	Flour
1/2 tsp	Salt
1/2 tsp	Baking soda

with

| 1/2 cup | Buttermilk |

Add:

| 1 tsp | Vanilla |

Pour into 2 prepared (buttered and floured) loaf pans.
Bake at 350 degrees for about 50 to 60 minutes.
Test with toothpick to see if done (toothpick comes out dry).

Cool completely.

*"My mother has been making breakfast...
one where we sit down to fresh orange
juice every morning..."*

TENDER AT THE BONE by RUTH REICHL

our notes:

When cooled slice very thinly.
Spread with butter or soft
cream cheese and put
another slice on top.
Cut in half or thirds, layer in
overlapping rows on a plate,
and serve. Delish!

your notes:

Questions

ONE

You can always glean something positive out of every situation.

What positive aspects did you feel existed between Ruth and her mom, dad, and brother?

TWO

What was your favorite story about Ruth's mom and her preparation of food for a party?

THREE

If Ruth tried to win people's acceptance by feeding them and showing them that she was an

exceptional cook, what do you think about the way she portrayed herself, especially with respect

to her teenage and young adult years?

FOUR

What did you think about the recipes that were included? Did you try any of them?

FIVE

Have you ever read one of Ruth Reichl's restaurant reviews? Is that a job you might enjoy?

June

SPORTS, TRAVEL, AND LEISURE

"The quality of the food is more important than convenience, and they will happily drive for an hour or more, salivating en route..." **A YEAR IN PROVENCE** by PETER MAYLE

This book is about a couple who finally realize their lifelong dream of living in France, where they pursue renovations on a two-hundred-year-old house they purchased in the Rhône Valley. Peter Mayle does a wonderful job of taking you along on their journeys and making you a part of the countless feasts they enjoy, both with their neighbors and on their own excursions in the country.

Suggestion

This month should be about relaxing and enjoying the company of your book club members, along with their significant other or a friend. We think having a backyard "Tailgate Party" will provide a subdued atmosphere where everyone can take it easy, discuss the book of the month leisurely, and enjoy some food and drink.

Menu

SERVES TEN TO TWELVE

Sangria

Assorted Beers and Sodas

Guacamole

Marinated Tri-Tip

Red Bell Pepper Potatoes

Grilled Asparagus and Mushrooms

Homemade Brownies

Our Review

A YEAR IN PROVENCE by PETER MAYLE

This book makes you want to drop everything and move to France, just as Peter Mayle and his wife did. A thoroughly enjoyable read in which Mayle's descriptions of his neighbors and the townspeople are brought to life in such a fashion that you feel an integral part of their experience.

Another interesting aspect was the entire saga of renovating their two-hundred-year-old farm house. Their dealings with contractors are described in an affectionate but humorous manner, and in such a way that you can completely identify with their anxieties. It's always interesting to learn how different cultures and nationalities try to accomplish similar tasks.

A YEAR IN PROVENCE revolves a great deal around food and drink, and whether or not you're hungry or thirsty, you will be every time you put this book down.

About the Author

Peter Mayle worked in the advertising business for fifteen years, starting out as a copywriter and continuing on as an executive. In 1975 he left Madison Avenue to pursue a career writing educational books for children. **A YEAR IN PROVENCE** was published in 1990 and became an international bestseller.

Suggested Readings

MIDNIGHT IN THE GARDEN OF GOOD AND EVIL by JOHN BERENDT

"...Emma stopped at the home of her ninety-year-old aunt to bring her a box of food she had taken with her from the country club."

THE ACCIDENTAL TOURIST by ANNE TYLER

"...they had Rose's pot roast, a salad with Macon's dressing, and baked potatoes."

THE MAN WHO ATE THE 747 by BEN SHERWOOD

"...savvy record seekers solved the nutritional problems with a straw, protein shakes, and Gatorade.

THE TOURNAMENT: A NOVEL OF THE 20TH CENTURY by JOHN CLARKE

"Aside from the removal of a woman named Violet Trefusis following an incident involving a Mars bar..."

HOW TO STAY ALIVE IN THE WOODS by BRADFORD ANGIER

"...nature will furnish every necessity...food, warmth, shelter, and clothing."

STANLEY KETCHEL by GENE SKYE

"...especially chocolate milk and candy which O'Connor believed to be a quick energy food and very nourishing."

Sangria

1 bottle	Merlot or red table wine
1 can	Diet 7-Up
1 can	Diet cherry 7-Up
1 cup	Orange juice
1 or 2	Oranges, sliced and halved

Reserve some orange slices for the individual glasses.
Mix all the ingredients in a large pitcher and serve over ice.

Guacamole

3	Avocados, peeled, pitted, and mashed
1/4 cup	Finely chopped onion
1/2 cup	Finely diced tomato
1 Tbs	Lime juice
1 tsp	Garlic salt
1 tsp	Pepper
2 Tbs	Sour cream

Combine all the ingredients and chill for 1 to 2 hours.
Serve with tortilla chips and deli salsa.

"...a sight that made me think of warm kitchens and well-seasoned stews, and it never failed to make me ravenous."

A YEAR IN PROVENCE by PETER MAYLE

our notes:

Additional beverages can be kept on ice in a shallow tin or tub, and guests can help themselves.

your notes:

Marinated Tri-Tip

2 lbs	Tri-tip (or London broil)
12 oz	Italian dressing
1/4 cup	Root beer
1/2 cup	Red zinfandel
1/2 cup	Beer
1/8 cup	Orange juice
2 Tbs	Worcestershire sauce
2 cloves	Garlic, minced
1 Tbs	Minced dried onion
1/4 tsp	Black pepper
1 tsp	Oregano

Mix all ingredients and marinate overnight, turning the meat occasionally.

Grill over medium-high fire for about 12 minutes on each side. Slice and lay on platter for serving.

"...a family restaurant of the kind that used to exist all over France before food became fashionable and bistros started serving slivers of duckling instead of daube and tripe."

A YEAR IN PROVENCE by PETER MAYLE

our notes:

Don't forget to sharpen your carving knife!

your notes:

Red Bell Pepper Potatoes

1 pound	Red skin potatoes
1	Red bell pepper, chopped
1 small	Onion, chopped
1 Tbs	Garlic salt
1 tsp	Pepper
1/2–1 stick	Butter
2 Tbs	Olive oil

Clean and wash potatoes, leaving skins on. Chop into small pieces and place in a 10 x 13-inch casserole dish. Mix in the chopped red bell peppers, onion, garlic salt, and pepper. Dot with butter and pour the olive oil over the mixture. Cover with foil and cook at 350 degrees for about 45 minutes, stirring halfway through the cooking time.

Grilled Asparagus & Mushrooms

1 lb	Fresh mushrooms
1 lb	Fresh asparagus
1 small	White onion, sliced (Vidalia, if in season)
1 Tbs	White wine vinegar
4 Tbs	Butter
1 Tbs	Garlic salt
1 tsp	Pepper

Combine all in aluminum grilling bag. Grill over medium heat for 20–25 minutes. Arrange on the same tray as the tri-tip, surrounding the meat with the vegetables.

our notes:

The potatoes also turn out great if cooked on the grill for about 45 minutes, using aluminum grilling bags.

Along the same note, you can place the vegetables in an ovenproof dish, cover, and bake at 350 degrees for about 30 minutes until tender but firm.

your notes:

Homemade Brownies

4 (1 oz)	Squares unsweetened chocolate
2/3 cup	Crisco® shortening
2 cups	Sugar
4	Eggs
1 tsp	Vanilla
1 1/4 cups	Flour
1 tsp	Baking powder
1 tsp	Salt
1 cup	Chopped walnuts

Preheat oven to 350 degrees. Grease a 9 x 13-inch pan.

In a saucepan melt the chocolate and shortening together. Once it is melted, remove from heat.

In a separate bowl, mix the sugar, eggs, and vanilla. Add to the melted chocolate. Add the remaining ingredients, stirring just until blended. Place in the prepared pan.

Bake about 30 minutes; do not overbake. Cool before cutting into bars.

"...with plenty of room in the middle for giant bowls of salad, pâtés and cheese, cold roasted peppers, olive bread, and chilled bottles of wine."

A YEAR IN PROVENCE by PETER MAYLE

our notes:

Another nice idea for a light dessert is fresh strawberries dipped in chocolate—these are easy to prepare and always look so pretty when you serve them.

your notes:

Questions

ONE

Did you feel that Peter Mayle described the characters and country in a way that immediately

engrossed you, or did it take you a while to warm up to his style?

TWO

If you've traveled to France or anywhere overseas, what type of practices did you find differ

greatly from the way things are done in the United States?

THREE

What was your reaction to the way Mayle described the various meals they experienced?

Did it inspire you to try some new dishes, or did it make you grateful for your last meal?

FOUR

Which excursion into the neighboring towns did you enjoy reading the most?

FIVE

After finishing the book, are you more or less inclined to pack up everything you own and

move to another country?

July
AMERICAN CLASSICS

"As I entered the kitchen, I sniffed a pleasant smell of gingerbread baking."

MY ANTONIA by WILLA CATHER

The novel, **MY ANTONIA**, is the story of Bohemian immigrant Antonia Shimerda, as lovingly told by her friend, Jim Burden, who was orphaned at an early age. Both arrived in Nebraska, their new home, at the same time. While Jim lived in comfort with his grandparents, Antonia's family struggled not only to adjust to farming in Nebraska but to life in America. In this novel, Jim recalls their childhood together as playmates and their adolescent years in the small town of Black Hawk, Nebraska.

Suggestion

Take advantage of the summer harvests with fresh vegetables and fruits.
Plan to have the meeting outside or on the porch.
Have a couple of bottles of Pellegrino or some other sparkling water on the table
for your guests to pour for themselves.

Menu

SERVES FOUR TO SIX

Sweet Wine

Veggies and Dill Dip

Garden Fresh Salsa

Spinach and Goat Cheese Salad

Italian Bread

Mixed Berries Parfait

Our Review

MY ANTONIA by WILLA CATHER

This book is an eloquent description of life in Nebraska in the late nineteenth century and a tribute to the pioneer women who lived during that time. Willa Cather's description of pioneer life and the harsh beauty of the Nebraska plains paints a vivid picture of the American West. One can't help but admire the character of Antonia. She remains positive despite the hardships she endures as she helps her family begin a new life on the prairie. There are many picturesque and memorable characters that attract you to the life and times of **MY ANTONIA**. The hardships and challenges pioneer women endured to make a home in the prairie will make one appreciate all the more what our ancestors endured to settle the West.

About the Author

Willa Cather was born in Virginia on December 7, 1873, and moved to Nebraska at the age of ten. She was educated at the University of Nebraska and upon graduation took an editorial job at a magazine in Pittsburgh. She ultimately settled in New York City in 1906 and accepted a position at *McClure's Magazine*. She was an award-winning writer of poetry, essays, and novels. **MY ANTONIA**, written in 1918, was one of her favorites. She died on April 24, 1947.

Suggested Readings

GONE WITH THE WIND by MARGARET MITCHELL

"On either side of her, the twins lounged easily in their chairs, squinting at the sunlight through tall mint-garnished glasses as they laughed and talked..."

TOM SAWYER by MARK TWAIN

"They built a fire... and then cooked some bacon in the frying pan for supper, and used up half of the corn "pone" stock they had brought."

COLD MOUNTAIN by CHARLES FRAZIER

"They cut the chickens up and fried them, cooked pole beans, boiled potatoes and stewed squash."

LONESOME DOVE by LARRY McMURTRY

"She made so many cakes that everyone got tired of them..."

HOUSE OF SEVEN GABLES by NATHANIEL HAWTHORNE

"...one containing flours, another apples, and a third, perhaps Indian meal."

CATCHER IN THE RYE by J. D. SALINGER

"...and had doughnuts and coffee."

Sweet Wine

Individual Servings: In a large, ice-filled goblet,
mix equal parts **cream soda** (yes—cream soda)
with **red wine** (use an inexpensive cabernet).
Place 3 or 4 thin slices of **peach** in the beverage and serve.

Veggies & Dill Dip

16 oz	Sour cream
2/3 cup	Mayonnaise
1 Tbs	Dill weed
1 Tbs	Dried parsley flakes
1 Tbs	Seasoned salt
1 Tbs	Accent
2 Tbs	Celery salt
2 drops	Worcestershire sauce

Combine all ingredients and refrigerate overnight.

Serve in a round bowl centered on a platter and surrounded
by colorful fresh vegetables.

"...and grandmother packed some loaves of
saturday's bread, a jar of butter, and
several pumpkin pies in the straw of the
wagon box."

MY ANTONIA by WILLA CATHER

our notes:

This sweet wine beverage
was mentioned in a
novel I was reading…
we just had to try it!

The Veggies and Dill Dip is a
recipe we've had for years.

your notes:

Garden Fresh Salsa

2 large	Ripe tomatoes, finely diced
1 small	Green pepper, finely diced
4	Scallions, thinly sliced
3 – 4 Tbs	Chopped green chilies (canned)
1/2 cup	Cilantro (leaves only)
1/2 cup	Olive oil
2 Tbs	Lemon juice
1 Tbs	Apple cider vinegar
1/2 tsp	Garlic powder
1 tsp	Salt
	Pepper to taste

Combine all ingredients and serve with tortilla chips.

"On sundays she gave us as much chicken as we could eat, and on other days we had ham or bacon or sausage meat."

"...she made my favorite pudding, striped with currants and boiled in a bag."

MY ANTONIA by WILLA CATHER

our notes:

This is best prepared a day in advance to let the flavors blend.

your notes:

Spinach & Goat Cheese Salad

1 lb   Smoked turkey breast, cut into bite-size pieces

Place in a salad bowl:

4 cups	Fresh spinach, cleaned and cut in bite-size pieces
3 oz	Goat cheese, crumbled
1/2 cup	Chopped fresh parsley
3 Tbs	Chopped fresh cilantro
1/4 cup	Toasted pine nuts

Dressing:

Cook **3 slices of bacon** in a fry pan. Set aside.
Reserve 2 Tbs of bacon drippings in the pan.

Add to the drippings:

1/4 cup	Red wine vinegar
1 tsp	Sugar
1/2 tsp	Salt
2 Tbs	Chopped tomatoes

Bring to a boil.

Toss the dressing with the spinach mixture, adding a little dressing at a time, so you don't use too much (there may be some left over). Add the turkey and crumbled bacon.

Serve with fresh Italian bread.

our notes:

Feta cheese can be substituted for the goat cheese.

your notes:

Mixed Berries Parfait

1 lg pack   Vanilla pudding (not instant), prepared as directed

2 cups   Fresh berries, cleaned and sliced if necessary
(raspberries, blueberries, strawberries)

Garnish: Sprigs of fresh mint

Starting and ending with the fruit, put alternating layers of pudding and fruit in parfait glasses. Garnish with a sprig of mint.

"The popcorn man wheeled his glass wagon under the big cottonwood by the door, and lounged in the sun..."

"...and he could make butter by beating the sour cream with a wooden spoon."

"... and when she came back from the kitchen she brought a bag of sandwiches and doughnuts for us."

MY ANTONIA by WILLA CATHER

our notes:

If you don't have parfait glasses, you can fill individual bowls with fruit, then place a large dollop of pudding in the middle and a berry on top.

your notes:

Questions

ONE

The book is called **MY ANTONIA**, but Jim describes other characters as well. Who is your favorite character

(besides Antonia) and why? Who is the most annoying character, and why does that person irritate you?

TWO

How was Antonia different from her parents and brother?

THREE

Do you think the story of the wolves and the wedding party is true? Did you find it very disturbing?

FOUR

While living and working at the Harlings', Antonia refused to give up her social life and lost her job because

of it. What direction would her life have taken if she had agreed to the Harlings' demands?

FIVE

Jim married a sophisticated and privileged woman who differs greatly from Antonia. Given his admiration for

Antonia, why do you think he married the woman described in the introduction?

August

ART, MUSIC, AND AWARD WINNERS

"Fresh squeezed, my lad. Make sure you squeeze it yourself and put lots of ice in the pitcher. I want it nice and cold."

THE ICE FLOE by J. TRACKSLER

This **2003 AMERICAN WRITERS AWARD WINNER** is the life story of a seemingly pleasant and accomplished woman who became a mercy killer at a very young age. It begins with her assisting her grandfather to die after he convinces her that it's the only compassionate thing to do. Interwoven is a murder mystery that can't help but get the reader's inquisitive juices flowing.
Definitely a thought-provoking and controversial book.

Suggestion

This month we focus on the creative talents of certain individuals, so we feel it's a perfect time to try some unique foods and perhaps a different atmosphere for your meeting. The Eggplant Spread, Tabbouleh, and Artichoke Rice Salad could be served in the center of the table with baskets of pita bread, giving it a more authentic setting.

Menu

SERVES FOUR TO SIX

Apricot Punch

Tabbouleh

Eggplant Spread

Pita Bread

Artichoke Rice Salad

Fruit Pizza

Tea

Our Review

THE ICE FLOE by J. TRACKSLER

The main character, Mallery Merrill, is charming, and even though certain sections are disturbing, you will find the book stimulating and interesting. Especially enjoyable is the way many twentieth-century experiences are presented as recollections.

Tracksler does a great job of including the reader by posing questions, as if Mallery were personally telling you the story. The stages of Mallery's life move along quickly, but with enough detail to leave the reader satisfied. In addition, **THE ICE FLOE** addresses mercy killing in numerous situations, explaining each time why the main character chooses to assist.

This book is guaranteed to generate a lively discussion!

About the Author

J. Tracksler was born and raised in Greenwich, Connecticut. She and her husband now live in Kittery Point, Maine, in a house that overlooks the ocean. Tracksler loves opera, good wine, and simple Italian food, and after a successful corporate career in human resources, she started writing stories. She is also the author of **THE BOTTICELLI JOURNEY** and **MURDER AT MALAFORTUNA.**

Suggested Readings

PALACE WALK by NAGUIB MAHFOUZ

"The oven room, although isolated...came alive with the delights of each holiday in its season, when hearts, merry with the joys of life, kept an anxious watch."

IN THE TIME OF THE BUTTERFLIES by JULIA ALVAREZ

"...an ordeal really, making that many little party sandwiches and the nephew and nieces not always showing up in time to help."

MUSIC & SILENCE by ROSE TREMAIN

"I had some moderate sport by drinking a vast quantity of wine and dancing until I fell onto the log pile..."

LIFE OF PI by YANN MARTEL

"I would start with rice and sambar."

THE HOURS by MICHAEL CUNNINGHAM

"she would fill the rooms of her apartment with food and flowers..."

GIRL WITH A PEARL EARRING by TRACY CHEVALIER

"I always laid vegetables out in a circle, each with its own section..."

Apricot Punch

Mix equal parts of apricot juice and lime-flavor sparkling water.
Pour over ice and garnish with sprig of mint.

Tabbouleh

1 cup	Chopped fresh parsley
1 cup	Couscous, prepared as directed
1	Tomato, seeded and finely diced
1 Tbs	Chopped fresh mint
2 Tbs	Fresh lemon juice
1/4 cup	Black olives, sliced (optional)

Salt and pepper to taste.

Combine all ingredients and chill.

Just before serving, add **2 Tbs of garlic** and **herb-flavor feta cheese** and mix lightly.

"And then I met Arnie Merrill. We were sitting next to one another at the Carnegie Deli, and we'd both ordered hot pastrami on rye."

THE ICE FLOE by J. TRACKSLER

our notes:

Always have ice tea available for those who aren't too adventuresome.

Using a clean scissors, snip off the stems of the parsley.

your notes:

Eggplant Spread

1 large eggplant, cut in half, pulp scooped out and shell discarded.
Cook the pulp in boiling water, about 5 minutes. Set aside.

In a large skillet place:

1/4 cup	Olive oil

Heat it up then add:

1	Green pepper, seeded and diced
2	Celery stalks, diced
1	Onion, diced
1	Carrot, finely chopped

Sauté about 3 or 4 minutes until tender.

Add:

1	Garlic clove, crushed
1 Tbs	Red wine vinegar
2	Tomatoes, seeded and chopped
2 Tbs	Chopped cilantro leaves (fresh is best)
1/4 tsp	Dried basil leaves
1 tsp	Salt
1/8 tsp	Cayenne red pepper
	Eggplant (from above)

Cook another 10 to 15 minutes until tender. Serve warm or cold.
Refrigerate it if you aren't serving it immediately.

"I felt an overwhelming desire to burst into tears, but managed to pour myself a cup of coffee and start to eat a croissant."

THE ICE FLOE by J. TRACKSLER

our notes:

This spread can be prepared the day before and refrigerated until ready to serve.

your notes:

Artichoke Rice Salad

1 pkg	Chicken-flavor Rice-A-Roni
4	Scallions or green onions, sliced
1/2 cup	Seeded and diced green peppers
12	Pimento olives, sliced
1 jar (14 oz)	Marinated artichoke hearts, cut into quarters (reserve 1/4 cup of the liquid)
1/2 cup	Mayonnaise
3/4 tsp	Curry

Cook the rice according to directions, then set in refrigerator to chill. Combine the scallions, green pepper, olives, and artichoke hearts in a large bowl. Add the chilled rice and mix gently. Put mixture into the dish you plan on using for serving. Combine the reserved liquid from the artichoke hearts, the mayonnaise, and the curry and drizzle over the rice dish. Serve chilled.

"We brought our coffee, cognac and two big slices of Nancy's Island Rum Coconut Cake..."

"Nancy's bulk came into the room carrying a big tray filled with soda and beer and whatnot."

THE ICE FLOE by J. TRACKSLER

our notes:

This looks pretty if you line the serving bowl with lettuce. If you decide to do this, make the rice and dressing ahead and chill them separately. Then, right before serving, line the lettuce bowl, fill it with the rice dish, and drizzle the dressing over all.

your notes:

Fruit Pizza

| 1 pkg | Refrigerated sugar cookie dough |
| | (available in grocery stores) |

Press into a 9 x 13-inch pan or cookie sheet. Bake according to directions on cookie dough package. Cool completely.

In a separate bowl blend:

3 oz	Cream cheese (brick type, not soft)
3 Tbs	Brown sugar
1 Tbs	Sour cream

Frost the cooled cookie dough with the blended mixture.

Place small pieces of fresh or canned fruit on top.

Fruit suggestions:

Strawberries, kiwi, blueberries, raspberries, mandarin oranges

"Evie Sullivan greeted me with more coffee and some freshly-made poundcake."

"She sipped at her coffee and made a face, then added a dollop of brandy..."

THE ICE FLOE by J. TRACKSLER

our notes:

This recipe is best if prepared the day of the meeting and refrigerated until served.

your notes:

Questions

ONE

What did you think about the title of the book?

Had you ever heard that term before?

TWO

Did you find it believable that a thirteen-year-old would actually be able

to kill her grandfather, even in the name of mercy?

THREE

Was the author able to convince you, or at least make you more open to the choices that

Mallory Merrill made in helping to end the lives of those sick and dying individuals?

FOUR

Did you have any inkling of who was the "Bandanna Murderer"?

And if so, at what point in the story did you figure it out?

FIVE

How did you like the ending? Is it what you expected?

september

INTERNATIONAL

> *"Also, in colorful steel platters are pieces of dark, sweet glutinous rice..."*

WHEN BROKEN GLASS FLOATS: GROWING UP UNDER THE KHMER ROUGE
by CHANRITHY HIM

This is an amazing and inspiring story about survival. Chanrithy Him lived through the occupation and takeover of her native land of Cambodia by the Khmer Rouge in the late 1970s. Having witnessed and survived unimaginable circumstances, Him feels a responsibility to tell the rest of the world about the atrocities, as well as the triumphs of the human spirit, that took place during that time.

Suggestion

Since the theme this month is international, it might be nice to inquire about the travel history and background of your fellow book club members. One idea is to have each person anonymously fill out a sheet of paper with a few questions such as, "Where are some of your favorite travel spots," "In what state or country did you attend school," etc. These sheets can be collected and read out loud for everyone to guess whom the answers belong to.

Menu

SERVES FOUR TO SIX

Hot Tea

Spiced Apple Cider

Pork Spring Rolls

Broc-Ramen Salad

Apple Torte

Our Review

WHEN BROKEN GLASS FLOATS: GROWING UP UNDER THE KHMER ROUGE
by CHANRITHY HIM

At first glance, this memoir may appear too sad and disturbing for most people, but in reality it is a heart-wrenching account of a person's will to survive. Knowing from the very beginning that Him does indeed survive, allows you to relive her experiences with a true sense of hope.

When Him was around ten years old, she was evacuated from Phnom Penh, and her life became a constant struggle just to stay alive. As Him moves to different villages and labor camps, the reader is completely drawn into every agonizing tribulation she encounters through her beautifully descriptive language. During these years, some of her surviving siblings are able to remain in contact and help each other to survive the mental and physical hardships they encounter. By the end of the book, Chanrithy Him is able to find some hope for the future and leaves the reader surprisingly optimistic.

About the Author

Chanrithy Him was born in Cambodia in 1965. She now lives in Eugene, Oregon, and works for the Khmer Adolescent Project, studying post-traumatic stress disorder among Cambodians. The term, **BROKEN GLASS FLOATS**, is derived from a Cambodian proverb that means the world is unbalanced.

Suggested Readings

GALILEO'S DAUGHTER by DAVA SOBEL

"Geppo bought bread for La Piera and himself..."

THE NO. 1 LADIES DETECTIVE AGENCY by ALEXANDER MCCALL SMITH

"The boy who makes the tea, the one with the hole in his brain..."

FOR WHOM THE BELL TOLLS by ERNEST HEMINGWAY

"...and if you passed your plate for stew, he cried,..."

LIFE AND DEATH IN SHANGHAI by NIEN CHENG

"...and every child in shanghai ate tomatoes either as a fruit or vegetable."

BELL CANTO by ANN PATCHETT

"But this visit, with its glorious birthday dinner replete with opera star..."

WHEN WE WERE ORPHANS by KAZUO ISHIGURO

"...to have the smells of food and incense come wafting towards me as I passed each brightly lit doorway."

Spiced Apple Cider

1 gallon   Apple cider
4 bags   Mulling spices (packaged like tea bags)

Pour cider into a pot on the stove. Once it comes to a simmer, add the spice bags and let the cider fill the air with its wonderful aroma.

Hot Tea

Have a few varieties of tea available. Serve with honey and lemon wedges.

"...two large spherical bamboo baskets are different Cambodian desserts wrapped in banana leaves."

"...Cambodian tradition, greeting guests with a sprawling bounty."

WHEN BROKEN GLASS FLOATS: GROWING UP UNDER THE KHMER ROUGE
by CHANRITHY HIM

our notes:

The cider could also be heated and kept warm in a Crock-Pot.

Garnish the steamed cider with cinnamon sticks for added appeal.

your notes:

Pork Spring Rolls

1 1/2 cups	Cooked and finely chopped or shredded pork
5 cups	Finely shredded cabbage
1 cup	Grated carrots
2 Tbs	Soy sauce
1/2 tsp	Ground ginger
1/4 tsp	Salt
1/4 tsp	Pepper
1 pkg	Egg roll wrappers
4 cups	Vegetable oil

Paste for wrappers: Equal parts flour and water. Start with 2 Tbs of each and make more as needed.

Combine pork, cabbage, carrots, soy sauce, ginger, and salt and pepper. Lay an egg roll wrapper on a flat surface with the point facing up. Place about 2 tablespoons of the mixture in the center. Bring the bottom point to the center, then the side points, keeping it compact. Finish rolling, using the flour and water paste on the top to seal.

To cook:
Heat the oil and deep-fry the spring rolls until golden brown. Remove and place on a paper towel to drain.

Makes approximately 12 to 14 rolls.

Serve with sweet and sour or soy sauce.

our notes:

These can be made ahead and stored in the refrigerator. When ready to reheat, put in an ovenproof dish, cover with foil, and place in a 350-degree oven for about 30 minutes, removing the foil for the last 10 minutes to regain crispness.

your notes:

Broc-Ramen Salad

1 pkg	Broccoli coleslaw, shredded
1 pkg	Top Ramen noodles, broken up
4	Green onions, thinly sliced
2 Tbs	Sesame seeds
1	Zucchini, cut in bite-size pieces

Dressing:

2 Tbs	Ketchup
1 Tbs	Hoisin sauce
2 Tbs	Sesame oil
6 Tbs	Vegetable oil
6 Tbs	White vinegar
4 Tbs	Sugar
1 tsp	Salt

Toss all of the ingredients together just before serving.

Alternative:

To serve as the main dish, add some cubed cooked chicken.

"Tha's way of finding out if the corn was sweet was to take a bite out of every cob..."

WHEN BROKEN GLASS FLOATS: GROWING UP UNDER THE KHMER ROUGE
by CHANRITHY HIM

The dressing can be made ahead and the other ingredients prepared, so all you have to do is toss everything together!

your notes:

Apple Torte

Preheat oven to 375 degrees.

Crust:

1/2 cup	Butter
1/3 cup	Sugar
1 cup	Flour
1/2 tsp.	Almond extract

Mix until crumbly. Press into 10-inch greased springform pan.

Filling:

8 oz.	Cream cheese
1	Egg
1/4 cup	Sugar
1/2 tsp	Almond extract

Combine all ingredients and spread over crust.

2	Apples, peeled and thinly sliced

Arrange apples over filling.

Topping:

1/4 cup	Sugar
1 tsp	Cinnamon
1/2 cup	Finely chopped walnuts

Spread topping over all. Bake for 35 to 40 minutes or until golden.

"Ra, ten, my shy sister who liked to help Mak cook and clean..."

**WHEN BROKEN GLASS FLOATS:
GROWING UP UNDER THE KHMER ROUGE**
by CHANRITHY HIM

Store in the refrigerator until just before your guests arrive.

your notes:

Questions

WHEN BROKEN GLASS FLOATS: GROWING UP UNDER THE KHMER ROUGE
by CHANRITHY HIM

ONE

How many of you had previous knowledge of the Khmer Rouge? Did you have any idea of the magnitude

of destruction and despair the Cambodian people suffered during this time?

TWO

When Him described certain events, particularly the deaths of her family members, did you feel she used too

much graphic detail, or the appropriate amount to enable her audience to envision the scene fully?

THREE

If you were in the same situation as that of Chanrithy Him, how long do you think

you would have been able to survive, especially with so little to eat?

FOUR

Do you think you would have taken the same risks as Him did to help your family members?

FIVE

After finishing the book, were you left with a sense of relief or a feeling of depression

or were you inspired and in awe of what people are capable of doing?

October

MYSTERIES

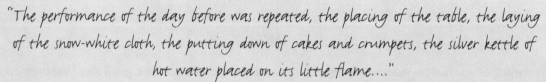

"The performance of the day before was repeated, the placing of the table, the laying of the snow-white cloth, the putting down of cakes and crumpets, the silver kettle of hot water placed on its little flame...."

REBECCA by DAPHNE DU MAURIER

This novel is about a timid young woman who marries a wealthy widower. From the moment they arrive at his ancestral home, she is haunted by the memory of his beautiful and talented deceased wife, Rebecca. The story is told by the second wife who is intimidated at first by Rebecca's memory and accomplishments. Once the real truth about Rebecca's life and death are revealed, the story takes a surprising turn.

Suggestion

As the days shorten in the fall and the weather changes, October seems like a good month to suggest suspense as the club's reading selections. You could offer a classic such as the one quoted above or go for something more current. Suspense novels are often on best-selling lists, but if you want to offer a variety don't forget to look to past publications.

Menu

SERVES SIX TO EIGHT

Cranberry Sparkler

Chicken Wraps

Squash Soup

Classic Green Salad with Shrimp and Balsamic Vinegar Dressing

Pumpkin Roll

Our Review

REBECCA by DAPHNE DU MAURIER

This is an intriguing book despite some preposterous turns of events. It is best characterized as a modern

gothic suspense since it includes mysterious elements as a brooding widower and violence and death that

take place on the estate of an aristocratic family. **REBECCA**, despite its dated clichés, will captivate you and

keep you in suspense as you follow the thoughts and actions of the heroine, the second Mrs. de Winter.

About the Author

Daphne du Maurier was born in England in 1907 to a wealthy and artistic family. She wrote several

novels and researched her family's genealogy as well. The setting for **REBECCA** was inspired by the beauty

of Cornwall, England, where du Maurier lived for several years. She was married to Lieutenant Colonel

Browning for thirty-three years and had three children. She died in 1989 at Kilmarth, her estate in Cornwall.

Suggested Readings

A IS FOR ALIBI by SUE GRAFTON

"I put in a filter paper and ground coffee... The gurgling sound was comforting..."

AN UNSUITABLE JOB FOR A WOMAN by P. D. JAMES

"she carried her shandy and the scotch egg to a seat against the wall..."

THE MURDER OF ROGER ACKROYD by AGATHA CHRISTIE

"He himself was engaged in brewing hot chocolate..."

WUTHERING HEIGHTS by EMILY BRONTË

...but I believe at Wuthering Heights the kitchen is forced to retreat altogether into another quarter.

THE SPY WHO CAME IN FROM THE COLD by JOHN LE CARRÉ

"..and topped them off with hot coffee."

"...and they'd finished the champagne..."

THE PILOT'S WIFE by ANITA SHREVE

"There were rock-hard bagels in a waxed paper bag on the table..."

Cranberry Sparkler

Mix equal parts:

Lemonade, cranberry juice, and club soda. Serve in a tall glass filled with ice and garnish with an orange slice.

Chicken Wraps

4 oz	Cream cheese (use a brick of cream cheese), softened
6 oz	Cooked chicken breast, diced
1/4 cup	Finely chopped onion
1 pkg	Crescent rolls
2 Tbs	Butter, melted
2 Tbs	Italian bread crumbs

Mix together first 3 ingredients. Open the container of crescent rolls, lay out the 4 rectangles (do not separate into triangles), then cut each rectangle into 4 squares. Place 1 tsp of mixture on each square, distributing the mixture as evenly as possible. Pinch the sides of each individual square closed over the mixture. Brush with butter, then sprinkle the bread crumbs over all. Place on ungreased cookie sheet and bake at 375 degrees for 11 to 13 minutes until golden brown. Makes 16 pieces.

"...Robert had offered him the cold soufflé for the second time."

REBECCA by DAPHNE DU MAURIER

our notes:

You can prepare the wraps in the morning, then cover with plastic wrap and refrigerate. Do not bake until just before serving.

your notes:

squash soup

3 lbs	Winter squash (butternut, acorn, banana, or turban)
1 1/2 cups	Chicken broth
1/2 cup	Water
1 cup	Chopped white onion
1/2 cup	Chopped carrots
1 tsp	Thyme, crushed
1/4 tsp	Pepper
2 oz	Half-and-half or whipping cream

Garnish: Parsley leaves

Halve the squash; remove the seeds and strings. Place the halves, cut side down, in baking dish. Bake at 350 degrees for 30 minutes. Turn cut side up. Continue baking 20 to 25 minutes until tender. Remove from oven and let cool. Once cooled remove pulp and discard the skin; set aside.

In another bowl combine the remaining ingredients, except the squash and half-and-half. Bring to a boil, simmer covered for 10 minutes, stir in squash and milk. Serve hot, garnished with parsley leaves.

"There was a little clutch of boiled eggs as well, in their own special heater, and porridge, in a silver porringer."

REBECCA by DAPHNE DU MAURIER

our notes:

This can be made a day ahead and reheated just before serving.

your notes:

Classic Green Salad with Shrimp

Salad greens:

Have a variety of greens for your salad, about 16 cups will serve 8 people generously. There are many to choose from: green and red leaf lettuces, romaine, butter or bibb lettuce, watercress, spinach, Belgian endive, mesclun leaves, or whatever fresh greens are available and appeal to you.

Lightly toss salad greens with your favorite Italian dressing. We recommend Newman's Own Balsamic Vinaigrette. Prepare individual portions of greens, arrange shrimp on top of salad, and garnish with **cherry tomatoes.**

Shrimp:

1 lb	Shrimp, cleaned and peeled
1 clove	Garlic, minced
2 Tbs	Olive oil
1 tsp	Parsley flakes or 1 Tbs fresh parsley leaves
2 Tbs	Lemon juice (preferably fresh)
2 Tbs	White wine
1 tsp	Lawry's Seasoned Salt

Combine all ingredients, except the shrimp, in a bowl. Add the shrimp and marinate overnight (about 8 hours). Place shrimp on cookie sheet and broil for about 15 minutes, turning once, until done.

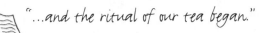

"...and the ritual of our tea began."

REBECCA by DAPHNE DU MAURIER

our notes:

Shrimp can be prepared the day ahead.

Scallops can be substituted for the shrimp.

your notes:

Pumpkin Roll

Cake:

3	Eggs
1 cup	Sugar
3/4 cup	Flour
1/2 tsp	Cinnamon
1 tsp	Baking soda
2/3 cup	Canned pumpkin

Beat eggs and sugar. Gradually fold in flour, cinnamon, and soda. Add pumpkin.

Pour onto jelly roll pan or cookie sheet that has been greased (or use Pam), lined with wax paper, and greased again. Bake at 375 degrees for 15 minutes. Cake should be springy. Turn baked cake out onto a towel sprinkled with **1/2 cup confectioners' sugar**. Remove wax paper, roll up in the towel and let cool.

Filling:

4 Tbs	Butter
16 oz	Cream cheese
1 1/2 tsp	Vanilla
2 cups	Confectioners' sugar

Beat together first three ingredients till fluffy, then add confectioners' sugar. Unroll cooled cake and spread with filling, then roll up and refrigerate for a few hours. Slice and garnish with **fresh fruit**.

our notes:

This dessert can be frozen for up to a month.

If you're ambitious you can prepare and freeze extra pumpkin rolls and then on the day of the book club give some to each member.

your notes:

Questions

ONE

The second Mrs. de Winter does not seem to have any self-confidence, and it only gets worse when she arrives at Manderley. Why wasn't Maxim more help to her?

TWO

Do you think Frank suspected that Maxim really killed Rebecca?

THREE

Were you satisfied with the description of Rebecca's behavior, and did it justify Maxim hating her enough to kill her?

FOUR

The second Mrs. de Winter said that everyone knew that Maxim killed Rebecca despite the fact that the doctor said she was dying. Do you think it is possible that she might have wanted to kill herself as the jury concluded?

FIVE

Does it surprise you that so many of the characters, including his new wife, appeared to support Maxim's words and actions blindly?

November

ADVENTURE

This is a journal of Richard Henry Dana's experiences as a sailor from 1834 to 1836. His sailing experience came about when, as a law student at Harvard—where he contracted measles, which affected his vision—he was advised to take a break from his studies to recover. He chose to join the crew of the *Pilgrim*, a merchant sea vessel, as an ordinary seaman. He kept a diary of his experiences as they sailed from Boston to California and back. His vivid accounts of the perilous trips around Cape Horn and accurate descriptions of the California coast made **TWO YEARS BEFORE THE MAST** an immediate bestseller in 1840. It is an authentic picture of the perilous life of a sailor in the early nineteenth century.

Suggestion

We tried to get away from traditional Thanksgiving menus to give everyone a break from turkey. You might consider asking the book club members if they would care to bring in a prayer or meditation for Thanksgiving to share with the group. Also, some families have special traditions they would be pleased to share.

Menu

SERVES FOUR TO SIX

Orange Iced Tea

Artichoke Dip or Fruit and Cheese Platter

Sausage, Shrimp, and Chicken Gumbo

Crusty French Bread

Bread Pudding

Our Review

TWO YEARS BEFORE THE MAST by RICHARD HENRY DANA

This fascinating narrative by Richard Henry Dana of life on the *Pilgrim* and the *Alert* gives a factual account of the daily activities of a common seaman during the 1830s. Although at times the details can be confusing to a nonsailor, it is interesting just to understand and appreciate the function of merchant ships and crews of that era. Dana's descriptions of the California coast and people are absorbing and captivating. It is well worth the read if for no other reason than to better understand and admire the dramatic life and times of a nineteenth-century seaman.

About the Author

Richard Henry Dana was born on August 1, 1815, in Cambridge, Massachusetts. When his vision was affected by measles, he was advised to take a break from school to improve his sight. He chose to sail as a common seaman rather than as a passenger or officer to learn about and document the experiences of sailors. His journey began in 1834 and resulted in **TWO YEARS BEFORE THE MAST**. Upon his return to Boston, he completed his studies and had a distinguished career in maritime law. He was also opposed to slavery and was a member of the Free Soil Party. He died in Rome from pneumonia on January 6, 1882, while working on a book about international law.

Suggested Readings

THE CALL OF THE WILD by JACK LONDON

"More of the white stuff was falling...then licked some up on his tongue..."

ROBINSON CRUSOE by DANIEL DEFOE

"...now I resolv'd to begin to use it freely, for my bread had been quite gone a great while."

DEBT OF HONOR by TOM CLANCY

"...with his usual two cups of morning coffee already at work..."

DAUGHTER OF FORTUNE by ISABEL ALLENDE

"...but it was aired in whispers in the kitchen with Mama Fresia..."

THE THREE MUSKETEERS by ALEXANDRE DUMAS

"As to D'Artagnan...he only found one breakfast of chocolate at the house of a priest of his own province."

GULLIVER'S TRAVELS by JONATHAN SWIFT

"The wife minced a bit of meat, then crumpled some bread on a trencher..."

Orange Iced Tea

2 quarts	Boiling water
4	Tea bags (black tea)
	Orange juice

Place tea in pot, pour boiling water over it and let steep for 5 to 10 minutes. Remove tea bags and let tea cool. Transfer to a pitcher once the tea is cooled and refrigerate.

To serve:
Put ice in individual glasses and fill half the glass with tea and the rest with orange juice. Stir and garnish with a slice of orange.

Artichoke Dip

1 large jar (14 oz)	Marinated artichoke hearts, drained and cut into small pieces
1/2 cup	Mayonnaise
1/2 cup	Grated Parmesan cheese

Blend the artichoke hearts and mayonnaise together. Place in shallow dish, approximately 8 inches round. Sprinkle Parmesan cheese over the mixture and bake in a preheated 350-degree oven for about 20 minutes until cheese is golden brown.

Serve hot with crackers. We recommend Carr's.

"...pitch all your sweetmeats overboard..."

TWO YEARS BEFORE THE MAST
by RICHARD HENRY DANA

our notes:

A nice lighter alternative or addition to the artichoke dip is simply putting out a fruit and cheese platter. We recommend trying some unusual cheeses such as Pesto Jack or Havarti with caraway seeds.

your notes:

Sausage, Shrimp, & Chicken Gumbo

1/3 cup	Vegetable oil
1/2 cup	Flour
4 cups	Chicken broth
1/2 tsp	Kitchen Bouquet (optional)
1 can (14.5 oz)	Stewed tomatoes
1 lb	Boneless, skinless chicken breasts, cooked and cut into bite-size pieces
1/2 lb	Sweet Italian sausage, cooked and cut into bite-size pieces
1 cup	Chopped okra
1 cup	Fresh parsley
1 tsp	Thyme
1 tsp	Sage
2 Tbs	Butter
1/2 cup	Chopped celery
2 cloves	Garlic
1	Onion, chopped
1	Green pepper, chopped
	Salt and pepper to taste
1 lb	Shrimp, medium size, shelled and deveined (precooked and frozen are also fine)
2 cups	White rice, cooked as directed

"...a pudding, or, as it is called, a 'duff'. This is nothing more than flour boiled with water, and eaten with molasses."

TWO YEARS BEFORE THE MAST
by RICHARD HENRY DANA

our notes:

Use leftover chicken with the skins and bones removed.

Zucchini can be substituted for the okra.

your notes:

sausage, shrimp, & Chicken Gumbo

CONTINUED

Heat oil in a large pot. Using a wire whip, add the flour, stirring constantly over low heat for about 5 minutes. Gradually add 4 cups of chicken broth, stirring until blended and smooth. Add Kitchen Bouquet. Add tomatoes, chicken, sausage, okra and herbs. Add cooked vegetables (see below).

Melt the butter in a small saucepan and add the celery, garlic, onion, and pepper. Cook vegetables about 10 minutes or until tender, stirring occasionally. Combine in one pot, then add 2 cups of water and heat to boiling. Reduce heat to low and simmer about 40 minutes. Add shrimp and cook, uncovered, about 5 minutes.

Mound hot rice in bowls and pour hot gumbo over it. Serve with crusty French bread. Delish!

"An hour is allowed for dinner, and at dark the decks are cleared up..."

"...living upon beef, hard bread, and frijoles, a peculiar kind of bean, very abundant in California."

TWO YEARS BEFORE THE MAST
by RICHARD HENRY DANA

our notes:

This may be prepared the day before and refrigerated. It can then be reheated in a Crock-Pot—just be sure to give yourself enough time!

your notes:

Bread Pudding

1 1/2 cups	Sugar
3/4 tsp	Cinnamon
3/4 tsp	Nutmeg
3	Eggs
3/4 tsp	Vanilla
3/4 cup	Coconut flakes (optional)
3/4 cup	Raisins
3/4 cup	Chopped pecans
5 Tbs	Butter, melted
3 cups	Whole milk, scalded
12 oz	Stale bread, no crusts

Mix together sugar, cinnamon, and nutmeg. Using a wire whisk, add eggs and vanilla. With a spoon, stir in coconut, raisins, and pecans. Add the butter, then the milk. Add the bread, mixing gently but thoroughly. Place in a 9 x 13-inch baking dish. Put in a cold oven; turn it to 350 degrees and bake for 1 hour until done.

You can serve the bread pudding warm as is or with a dab of whip cream or the whiskey sauce below.

Whiskey Sauce (Optional):

1/4 cup	Butter	Cook ingredients over a low heat until they thicken, about 5 minutes. Remove from heat and add 2 Tbs whiskey.
1/2 cup	Sugar	
1	Egg yolk	
2 Tbs	Water	

When you add the whiskey, the sauce will flare up a bit, so remove the pan from the stove top before you add it.

Questions

TWO YEARS BEFORE THE MAST by RICHARD HENRY DANA

ONE

Describe the kind of man Richard Henry Dana would be and what kind of occupation

he would have if he lived today.

TWO

Richard Henry Dana described the unreasonable and irrational behavior of the captain in a chapter titled,

"Flogging." Was the author justified in doing nothing to help the men?

THREE

The Sandwich Islanders were described as "the most interesting, intelligent and kindhearted people"

he ever fell in with. Do you believe a person's culture can determine his or her actions and behaviors?

FOUR

Forgetting gender, would you have been able, at age eighteen, to do what the author did?

FIVE

If you were able to interview Richard Henry Dana today, what would you ask him?

December

INSPIRATIONAL

"We would hide food from one another, squirreling away a precious grilled cheese or fried bologna sandwich..."

THE COLOR OF WATER: A BLACK MAN'S TRIBUTE TO HIS WHITE MOTHER
by JAMES McBRIDE

Written from the vantage point of two people, this book covers the life of James McBride's mother, an Orthodox Jew whose childhood was difficult and disturbing. Interspersing tales of his own background, he describes what it was like to be raised in a family of twelve with a black father and a white mother, financially poor, and having to deal with race-related issues. It's a beautiful tribute, exemplifying the power of love and the amazing feats people can accomplish with determination and the right mind-set.

Suggestion

It's been about six months since you've last had your members bring a guest, so in the spirit of the season, we think it's the perfect time to have a party to which all the significant others are once again invited. For a holiday party we feel it's best to stick with dishes that are easy for people to eat as they circulate and socialize. A fun idea to keep your guests entertained is to have each person bring a wrapped gift to exchange. Have everyone place the presents in the center of the group, then give each guest a playing card. The host, using a second deck of cards, calls out the cards one at a time and then waits for each guest with a matching number to choose a present from the center. When those disappear, guests start taking a gift from anyone they choose—and that's when it really gets interesting!

Menu

SERVES TEN TO TWELVE

Eggnog with or without Brandy
Pinwheel Sandwiches
Cheese Tortellini Salad
Zucchini Bites
Almond Tea Cakes

Our Review

THE COLOR OF WATER: A BLACK MAN'S TRIBUTE TO HIS WHITE MOTHER
by JAMES McBRIDE

James McBride did a wonderful job alternating between his mother's background and his own upbringing. As the story progresses, we learn about his mother, which helps to explain her convictions and her many eccentricities. His mother's background, presented in an interview format, helps the reader become completely engrossed in her life.

Being the eighth of twelve children, McBride covers a vast array of interesting events that took place at home with his siblings and in the outside world. His mother was a hard worker who was strict and focused on instilling her strong beliefs that God and education were of utmost importance. **THE COLOR OF WATER** is the answer to James's question about what color God is—what a great answer! The book directly addresses many racial issues that continue to this day. If we're truly going to get past the frictions between varying ethnic backgrounds, we need to be aware of and address the numerous issues presented in this book.

McBride's mother truly lived by her convictions, and although the family had many struggles, financially and emotionally, she raised a family of twelve educated and aspiring children, a remarkable accomplishment on any front.

About the Author

James McBride studied composition at The Oberlin Conservatory of Music in Ohio, received a master's degree in journalism from Columbia University, and is an award-winning musician. He is a former staff writer for the *Boston Globe*, *People*, and the *Washington Post*, and his articles have appeared in numerous newspapers and magazines. He has appeared on several national radio and television shows as well.

Suggested Readings

BRUSH OF AN ANGEL'S WING by CHARLIE W. SHEDD

"On my very first Sunday, I had chicken at Grandma Minnie's."

THE PROPHET by KAHIL GIBRAN

"...if you bake bread with indifference, you bake a bitter bread that feeds but half a man's hunger."

THE FIVE PEOPLE YOU MEET IN HEAVEN by MITCH ALBOM

"...skipping his routine of picking up his bagel and a soft drink for breakfast."

THE LOVELY BONES: A NOVEL by ALICE SEBOLD

"Grandma Lynn had made him a skillet-sized peanut butter pancake..."

KITCHEN TABLE WISDOM: STORIES THAT HEAL by RACHEL NAOMI REMEN

"In her odd intense way she told me that the plum suffered because it was the first, it bloomed early, in February, often still in winter..."

THE ALCHEMIST: A FABLE ABOUT FOLLOWING YOUR DREAM
by PAULO COELHO, TRANSLATED by ALAN R. CLARKE

"But we could sell tea in crystal glasses."

Eggnog

For every 6 oz. glass of eggnog add 1 shot of brandy.
Sprinkle with nutmeg.

Pinwheel sandwiches

1 pkg	Cracker bread (this can usually be found near the bakery department—looks similar to tortilla shells, but larger)
8 oz	Cream cheese, softened
1 can	Black olives, chopped
1 jar	Pimentos, chopped
1 bag	Baby spinach leaves, stems removed
1 pkg	Ham, sliced in 1- or 2-inch squares

On one piece of cracker bread, spread cream cheese over two-thirds of the bread, starting on the left side. Sprinkle the black olives, pimento, spinach leaves, and ham on top of the cream cheese.

Beginning with the left side, roll tightly into a log shape. Cut into 1/2-inch slices. I usually cut the log in half and work my way from there. The ends are usually reserved for taste testing!

"...the wholesalers used to sell margarine without the yellow in it, so I'd have to go in the back and add the yellow dye to it..."

THE COLOR OF WATER by JAMES McBRIDE

our notes:

Arrange sandwiches on a bed of lettuce. For color, scatter a few cherry tomatoes around the pinwheels.

your notes:

Cheese Tortellini Salad

1 lb	Cheese tortellini
1 bottle	Italian dressing
1/4 cup	Grated or shredded fresh Parmesan cheese
1 bag	Baby spinach, stems removed
1	Red bell pepper, cut into bite-size pieces
1 small bag	Slivered almonds

Cook the tortellini according to package directions. Pour the dressing over the warm tortellini. Mix in the Parmesan cheese and refrigerate overnight.

Just before your guests arrive, add the spinach, bell pepper, and almonds to the marinated tortellini.

"I dove under an abandoned dump truck and lay quiet, still clasping a bottle of cheap, peppermint-tasting wine..."

THE COLOR OF WATER by JAMES McBRIDE

our notes:

The spinach and bell pepper can be prepared ahead so you can just toss everything together right before serving.

your notes:

Zucchini Bites

3 cups	Sliced zucchini
1 cup	Bisquick
1/2 cup	Chopped onion
1/2 cup	Grated Parmesan cheese
2 Tbs	Chopped parsley
1/2 tsp	Salt
1/2 tsp	Oregano
1/2 tsp	Black pepper
1 clove	Garlic, minced
1/2 cup	Vegetable oil
4	Eggs, slightly beaten

Grease a 13 x 9 x 2-inch pan. Mix all ingredients and place in the pan. Bake at 350 degrees for about 25 minutes, or until golden brown. Cut into small squares—about 8 across and 5 down—to make 40 bite-size pieces.

"He'd come into her factory office twice a week and they'd smooch it up, and have wine and cheese and crackers."

THE COLOR OF WATER by JAMES McBRIDE

our notes:

Set the squares on the plate shingle-style and decorate with whole black olives.

your notes:

Almond Tea Cakes

1 cup	Margarine or butter, softened
1/2 cup	Confectioners' sugar
1 tsp	Almond extract
2 1/4 cups	Flour
3/4 cups	Finely chopped almonds
1/4 tsp	Salt
	Confectioners' sugar

Heat oven to 400 degrees. Mix margarine, 1/2 cup confectioners' sugar, and almond extract. Stir in the flour, nuts, and salt until dough holds together. Shape into 1-inch balls and place about 1 inch apart on an ungreased cookie sheet. Bake 10 to 12 minutes or until set but not brown.

Roll in confectioners' sugar while warm. Cool, and then roll in sugar again.

"My husband cooked better than I did, and when I stayed home after our first baby I had to learn to cook from my black friends..."

THE COLOR OF WATER by JAMES McBRIDE

our notes:

When serving, place a few strawberries and/or grapes in the center of a platter and surround with the tea cakes.

your notes:

Questions

ONE

Were you surprised that James's mother was able to take her children to so many cultural events,

given their dire financial situation?

TWO

What did you think about Ruth McBride's style, using a queen and king hierarchy,

of managing the children at home?

THREE

Would you have been as strong as Ruth and ignore the stares and comments that people made?

FOUR

Do you have any friends or acquaintances who had parents of different ethnic or religious backgrounds?

What issues did they encounter growing up?

FIVE

Is there someone you've come across in your life whom you've found to be extraordinarily inspiring?

Index

Soup & Salads

Pasta, Side Dishes, & Miscellaneous

Meat & Seafood Dishes

Desserts